Animals
are
MIRACLES

By Steven A. Guemann
Illustrations by Jared Murnan and Steven Guemann
Clipart by Nova Development Corporation

To Barbara, Rebecca and Carrie

"Are not two sparrows sold for a cent? And yet not one
of them will fall to the ground apart from your Father."

Mathew 10:29

CONTENTS

Forward

Animals are Miracles, Book 1, is the first in a series *of* rhymed stories about some of the world's most well-known and loved animals. Most of the personal anecdotes accompanying the stories are based on actual experiences of the author, his children and grandchildren. It is recommended that these stories be read to young children as part of a family time. Children are encouraged to guess the words that are highlighted in blue, based on the rhyming pattern and on the sense of the narrative. It is the author's hope that these stories will be both informative and fun and that they will bring the reader and the listener closer to the Creator through the wonders of the creation. Each animal is, indeed, a miracle, to be enjoyed and preserved for future generations.

Introduction

Did you know that miracles are present all around you? You'll see them in each animal in ways that may astound you! Imagine live piñatas in a thousand shapes and sizes, each one with a colored coat and full of great surprises! Indeed there are so many, with such variety, that most we'll only read about and never get to see! Some come dressed in feathers, some in fur or scales. Other ones come armor-clad or housed in fancy shells.

A world without the animals would be a dreary place, like sunsets without color or food without the taste! I'd rather give up flowers and all the stars on high than watch the animals depart and have to say good-bye! Yes, living without animals would be a sorry fate, for animals are gifts of God and tell us of His grace. If God cares for the sparrow that falls upon the ground, then certainly His love for us does even more abound!

Each creature is quite special and really like no other, and when the final one is gone there'll never be another! How sad that some don't treasure them, as blessings from above, not as objects to be used, but creatures to be loved! Remember, every animal, no matter great or small, is like a living miracle created for us all. Even little beetles, designed with grace and art, bid us kneel in humble praise: "Oh, God, how great Thou art!"

Pampered Pets

The Cat

To start our tale of animals, let's play a little game.* I'll describe a house pet and you can guess its name! This pet moves like a shadow; he doesn't make a sound. And often, when you think he's near, he's nowhere to be found. One moment he is at your feet, the next you find he's not. Then, just when you decide he's gone, he's on your lap: KERPLOP! I think you may have guessed by now just what I'm driving at, but should it be I've stumped you, I'm thinking of a cat!

Some people say they don't like cats because they have bad habits, but I would rather teach a cat than try to train a rabbit! A cat is so much better than whatever might come next, for rabbits are unteachable and squirrels are but a pest! And though they're not like loving dogs, they're rarely ever mean, and unlike dogs that make a mess a cat is super clean.

A cat will purr and cuddle up, but don't let these things trick you. If he were your size, and you his, he'd sooner eat than lick you! The only thing that saves you from being eaten is your size, so just because your cat is tame, don't think he's civilized! And cats all have a habit that sometimes gets me down: They're fond of catching little things and batting them around. My parents always taught me that this is very rude; "Eat what's placed before you, and don't play with your food!"

Still, cats are very handy if your problem is a mouse, but don't expect much more of them; they won't protect your house! They're awfully cute and cuddly and can be lots of fun, but when you need a Rin Tin Tin, you've got a Run-Tom-Run!

*Before showing the pictures at the beginning of each story, allow the child to guess the animal being described.

Quick Paw

Our neighbor had an old, white cat with pinkish, padded paws who, when provoked, thought it no joke, and countered with her claws! If you merely touched her tail, your finger she'd harpoon, punctuating her distain with tiny puncture wounds!

An old man came to visit once, who thought himself quite smart and who, despite his ninety years, was still a boy at heart. I saw him try to tease that cat, thinking he was faster. With muffled cry he jumped so high, I thought he'd met his Master!

And when he came back down again, on landing where he sat, he said to me with sheepish grin, "You can't outdraw a cat!" I couldn't help but smile inside; I guess it served him right. You shouldn't choose a feisty cat with whom to pick a fight! Now while I don't like fighting, and envy neither one, I hope that when I'm old like them I, too, can still have fun!

Wild Cats

I can still remember, when I was just a child, we came upon some kittens born out in the wild. My father, being a kind man, with children of his own, decided he would round them up and find them all a home. He fought a dozen skirmishes and battled all that day, and what he looked like afterwards I wouldn't want to say! But should you try to do the same, there's one thing you should know: He came back smelling very bad and scratched from head to toe!

That day I learned a lesson that I will not forget: Don't confuse wild animals with a domestic pet! They look alike in every way and yet they're miles apart. Appearance is deceptive; you are what's in your heart!

Little Angel

I can still remember, though it happened long ago, my sister got a kitten with fur like powder snow. She called him Little Angel, a choice that seemed just right. I'd never seen a cat like that; his face was halo bright! But names can be deceptive and soon it was apparent that Angel liked to wander off, a sort of kitten errant. Of course, all cats are curious, that needs no explanation, but Angel's knack for getting lost defied imagination!

We were all inside one day, just as you are now, when suddenly, from somewhere, we heard a faint meow. It sounded somewhat muffled and rather hard to hear. A plaintive little cry it was, far off and yet quite near. And so we started looking; we searched both up and down. But after half an hour no Angel could be found. He wasn't in the cupboards, nor under couch or chair, nor hidden under covers, or in closets anywhere. Now just in case you think this strange or question if it's true, you must put on your thinking cap; I'll give you one more clue. That cat was somewhere in the house and yet he really wasn't. How can that make perfect sense, when it seems it doesn't?

And then a thought occurred to me: If we called out his name, he might respond and we could tell from where the answer came. I thought we'd make a game of it to see if we could hear him. Like playing Marco Polo, we'd know when we got near him. We called him and we listened and all at once I knew! I ran up to the fireplace to check the chimney flue! With head beneath the damper, I opened it a crack and saw a blackened nose pop out! We'd found our mystery cat! Now how he ever got up there we never, ever knew. Did he topple down the chimney or hop into the flue? However Angel did it, his name took on new meaning: Should we call him "Fallen Angel" or rename him "Great Houdini?"

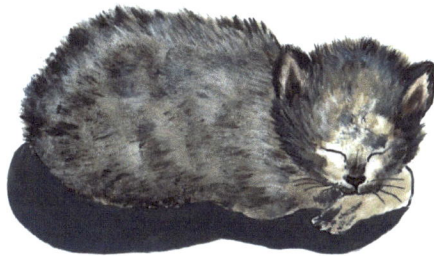

Vanishing Rewards

One summer, many years ago, when I was feeling down, my mother promised me a pet and took me to the pound. We went to get a kitten, a cat to call my own. I'd always have a playmate and never feel alone!

Now as we went from cage to cage to find the perfect cat, we spied an old, gray tabby, as large as he was fat! But when my mother called to him, at once he stood erect and, running, jumped into her arms and hugged her 'round the neck! I think that you can understand, my mother was so smitten, she promised me a hamster if I'd just give up the kitten! I guess you know, she got her way; we went home with the tabby, and soon I had my hamster and everyone was happy!

But late one day he got a way, and just as quick as that, my hamster prize was rounded up and eaten by the cat! I'd made a bad decision and now I had to pay. The very cat that got me him had taken him away!

That day I learned a lesson: When feeling pressed or pushed, never trade a kitten for a hamster in the bush! And yet I'm glad this little tale came to a happy end: I finally got my kitten and our tabby got a friend!

The Dog

All animals are special, but in the very end, I think you will agree with me that dogs are man's best friend! No other creature, large or small, can match the things they do; they'll bring your slippers, guard your house and even comfort you. Their nose is good at finding things that men could never find, and with their eyes and ears they serve as guide dogs to the blind. That leaves their feet for sleds and sheep, and now you understand why dogs that walk on padded paws are also helping hands!

A dog is quite intelligent regardless of his mix, and if you train him when he's young, he'll quickly learn new tricks. But what makes dogs so special, besides the tricks they know, are all the ways they mimic us through feelings that they show. They're really quite expressive and lead with their emotions, and best, you know they're happy when you see their tail in motion. But when their tail stops wagging, or hangs between their legs, they're either feeling guilty or they're sad or just afraid. Some say cats are friendlier but that cannot be true, for dogs are like the sunshine, while cats are like the moon. A dog bestows his love on all and comes when he is needed, while cats reflect the love they get and spurn you when mistreated! I think that's why dogs often try to jump and lick my hand. No matter how I feel or act, they love me as I am! I heard a little prayer once, spoken by a man: "Lord, help be the kind of person my dog thinks I am!"

While dogs cannot match people, who reason and can talk, they understand all languages and seem to read out thoughts! Be it English, French or German, Spanish or Chinese—they'll shake your hand, roll over and do just as you please.

I heard a Frenchman speaking once to a German Dachshund. He kept on shouting "Au Pied!"* while the dog just watched him. I thought, "Now, that's ridiculous; what good is your command? When you speak in French like that, no one can understand!" But then I thought, "That's silly! It's true that dogs can't talk, but as for understanding they're little polyglots!"

*"Heel!"

8

Justice

I knew a giant Labrador; Justice was his name. He loved to go on hunting trips to fetch and bring back game. Now when the hunting season passed, he turned to chasing balls. He'd bring them back a hundred times and tire not at all! I'd throw for half an hour, and think, "Now this is it!" But then he'd find new energy; it seemed he'd never quit!

That dog could run for hours, without a moment's rest! I thought, "My word, this is absurd! I think this dog's obsessed! No matter how I threw it, or hit it with a bat, he knew just where that ball would land and always brought it back. I thought, "Perhaps a cannon that shoots balls half a mile would keep him running long enough to let me rest awhile!"

I finally picked the ball up and threw it in the lake. I thought, "Now this will end it! Enough, for goodness sake!" But Labradors are swimmers and soon I came to see, no matter where I threw that ball it would come back to me!

That day I learned a lesson. I say this part in jest: Never start a contest with a dog that is obsessed! I might have thought it at the time but now I truly know: I didn't teach that dog to fetch; he taught me how to throw!

9

The Guinea Pig

Guinea pigs are animals that look a little funny, something like a cross between a dust mop and a bunny. They look the same at both extremes sometimes, without knowing, it's hard to tell, when they stand still, which way that they are going!

Now why we call them guinea pigs is still unknown to many, since guinea pigs are neither pigs nor creatures from New Guinea. Perhaps because they make a squeal, though really it's a squeak, somewhat like a noisy wheel or like a door that creaks.

Now if you think you're old enough to have one of your own, remember that a guinea pig does not do well alone. You have to feed him every day and clean the cage each week, for guinea pigs drink all day long and soon the cage will reek! And when you clean the cage out, and bring your pet outside, never leave him in the sun, for heat they can't abide!

My sister had two guinea pigs. She called them Fluff and Flipper. I almost put one on one night; I thought it was my slipper! I quickly learned the difference and now I've got it right: Guinea pigs let out a squeal and slippers do not bite! I'm glad I didn't grab him before he squealed and scampered, or nabbed him like a dirty sock and tossed him in the hamper!

The Cockatiel

My father bought a cockatiel, a precious little thing. And Oh, the tunes that he could tweet and songs that he could sing! At first he simply sat and stared; he didn't say a word. It seemed like he was very shy, a bashful little bird!

I named him Little Chico Boy and talked to him each day. I'd say his name and listen, to hear what he would say. At times I thought he'd never learn; it wasn't meant to be. But then, one day, I whistled and he whistled back at me! From that day on, and all day long, he matched me song for song. Tune for tune and note for note, he rarely got it wrong! From marching songs to reveille, 'twas really quite a feat. I'd never heard a bird like that; he rarely missed a beat!

And then one day it happened, much to my dismay. My father left a door ajar and Chico flew away! We searched all I day to find him, and looked up every tree. I called his name a thousand times: "Chico, come to me!" But Chico was quite happy far up in the sky. In all his little bird life he'd never flown so high! And though I don't know where he flew, I'll never think him stranded. Instead I'll always picture him at home just where he landed. And should you chance to see him, I don't know where or when, be sure to give a whistle back; you might have found a friend!

Corn Snakes

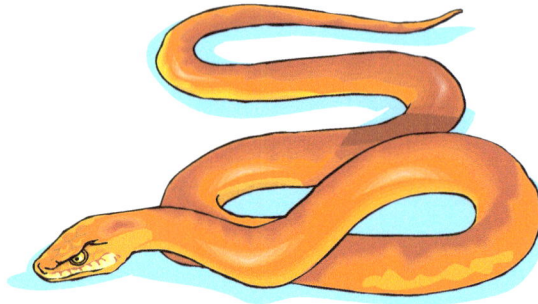

Snakes are not a cuddly pet, and yet, there is a type that bears the name "constrictor," and loves to squeeze you tight! I saw one in a movie once attack an alligator. He wrapped him up from stem to stern and mashed him like a 'tater!

While large ones are quite dangerous, and pose for all a threat, little ones, like corn snakes, are often prized as pets. My parents let me have one, a fascinating thing, twelve inches long from tip to tail and colored rosy pink. At night I'd take him out to play and place him on my arm. He liked to curl around my neck, too small to cause alarm. They really are quite friendly, when bred and raised as pets, and if you give them time and love they're even nicer yet! And corn snakes aren't a lot of work; they need just light and heat. And best of all, their feeding time is only once a week! But should you wish to get one, remember this advice: As cousins to the rat snake, they live on pinkie mice! You buy them freshly frozen, then take them out to thaw, soak them in warm water, and serve them to him raw!

Now if your mother's squeamish or of fragile disposition, she might not like the sight of mice floating in her kitchen. I put one in a bottle once, and left it in the sink, and when my mother shook it out, it pushed her o'er the brink!

12

She told me she could take no more and, picking up her phone, she called the local pet store to find that snake a home. But sometime between bedtime and just before the dawn, my corn snake slithered out his cage; by morning he was gone! I thought it was my mother's fault. She said I shouldn't talk; it never would have gotten loose had I secured the lock!

We never, ever came to know just how it got away, nor how it managed to survive for almost twenty days! We checked in every corner, every square inch of the floor, but after several weeks assumed he'd slithered out the door. Now just when we had lost all hope of knowing where he hid, my kitten, who was now a cat, looked underneath the fridge! It's strange, it took a little cat; we really should have known! That snake had found the warmest spot in our entire home!

And so, with mixed emotions, first joy and then dismay, I welcomed back my corn snake, and my mom gave him away! And though I wasn't happy, I'd made a big mistake. It takes more than good feelings in caring for a snake. I'm glad it has a happy home, and yet I feel the loss. You really shouldn't get a pet until you count the cost! Next time you beg your parents for a pet your very own, remember pets do not do well on promises alone!

The Goldfish

The goldfish spends his lifetime in a bowl with just one view, yet every time he goes around he finds it all quite new! He doesn't know a lot of tricks, apart from blowing bubbles, a rather uneventful life but free of care and troubles! Indeed, I sometimes envy him when swimming in our pool. He gets to stay and play all day while I go off to school. But when I come back home again, I quickly change my mind. I'd rather be at work in school than bored and left behind!

The Midas Touch

When I was only eight years old one sunny day in June, I won a goldfish at the fair for popping three balloons. Now after buying a fishbowl with colored rocks and sand, my mother, who loved projects, devised a bigger plan. She started with her nicest smile and waved her magic wand, and asked my dad to be a sport and build our fish a pond! At first her magic didn't work, but after several days my father had a change of heart and saw it mother's way. He dug with pick and shovel, just like a seasoned miner, and in two days produced a pond with filter, pump and liner! And though the total price tag seemed awfully high to me, I thought I should remind my dad: We got the fish for free!

Now fishponds are a lot or work and though they do look nice, should you decide to have one, too, remember this advice: You have to skim the leaves off and keep the filters clean, and, even then, the odds are great your water will turn green. At first our pond was crystal-clear and things were going fine, but soon the warmer days arrived and with them algae slime! We tried in vain to pull it out, then chose another tactic, pouring algae-killer in to stop and counteract it.

Now, should you ever do the same do not be too ambitious, lest the outcome you achieve surpasses all your wishes. Indeed, I'm sad to have to say we got more than our wish; the treatment killed the algae off and also took my fish! My father took it pretty hard. He'd labored several days, to see the time and money spent sprout wings and fly away! And though I never put my trust in gold or worldly things, I learned that day, to my dismay, that goldfish, too, have wings!

The good news is that goldfish are easy to replace, and soon I had three more of them swimming in its place. From one to three in just one day, that might not sound like much, but when it came to goldfish, I had the Midas touch!

Things with Wings

15

The Bat

Can you name an animal that sleeps while upside down, has wings to fly just like a bird, is blind, yet "sees" by sound? An animal that lives in caves and leaves to hunt by night? If you guessed a bat, my friend, you're absolutely right!

Deep in Carlsbad Cavern, close up against the ceiling, hang half a million sleeping bats just waiting for the evening. When daylight finally turns to dusk, they wake alert and ready to burst forth from the cavern's mouth like clouds of swirled confetti!

To name the different types of bats is anything but easy, for bats make up a family of a thousand different species, from tiny little microbats as small as they are cute, to giant, swooping megabats that live off game and fruit. Many look like creatures that live inside your house. In fact, in many languages they're called a flying mouse! I think that's far more picturesque than calling him a bat, but both surpass in taste and class a name like flying rat!

The bat is a magician, and let me tell you why: He doesn't need to see a thing to know just where to fly. The sound he makes hits everything that ventures through the air, and when it bounces back to him it tells him what is there!

Because he cannot launch himself, like birds, from off the ground, he simply falls from where he roosts and hang-glides all around. And when he flaps his jointed wings, from which he gains his fame, the bat can stop in mid-air flight and head back where he came. I saw one fly by after dusk and watched from where I sat. He did a double loop de loop, an aerial acrobat! He seemed to flitter as he flew and as he fluttered by, I said, "My word, is that a bird or some strange butterfly?"

Now when you see him change his course and zigzag through the sky, you know he's after insects, to catch them on the fly. A bat can live most anywhere where insects can be found, so when you see an insect, know that bats are hanging 'round! It truly is amazing that in a single night three thousand bugs fall victim to his giant appetite! I wish that they were pancakes and I could eat like that! I'd finish off a thousand of them in a single stack!

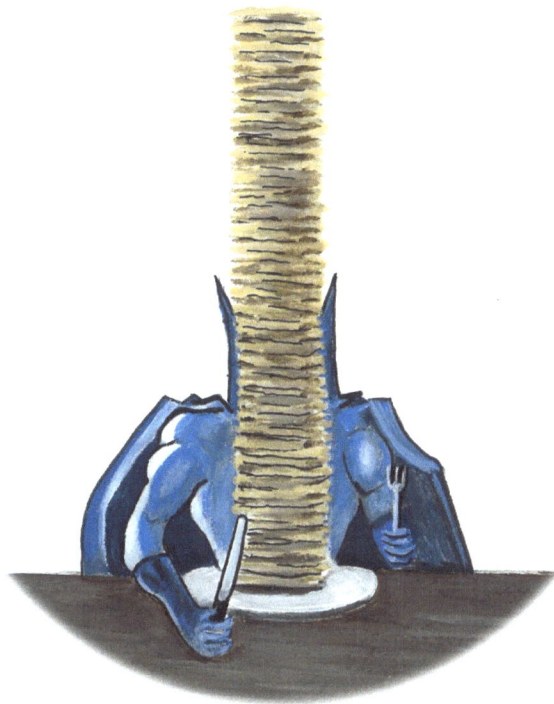

The Bee

The bee, of all the insects, is truly man's best friend. He works with farmer dawn to dusk and then begins again. Of all the insects, large and small, in all of God's creation, none other is so vital in the task of pollination. While tractors may replace the horse and airplanes copy birds, while great machines may mimic moles and bore throughout the earth, while ships may dive like dolphins and tame the deepest sea, no power on earth can match this little bug we call the bee.

I've heard that he is stronger than any bug around. They say he'll lift a full grown man six inches off the ground! But though he packs a wallop, don't let that cause alarm. He only wants to do his job and really means no harm. Without the bee the blossomed tree would wither and retreat and animals and man himself would have no food to eat. Yes, honeybees are wonderful and not just for their honey. How sad that people step on them and think that it is funny!

But hornets are a different thing and little joy they bring. Instead they seem to be content to bite you and to sting! They'll smell a roasting chicken from a thousand feet away, and just when you sit down to eat they're on you for the day!

Hornet Pie

When I was playing in a field with no one else around, I spied a string of yellow jackets coming from the ground. I told my neighbor, Sally, and we devised a plan to rid the playfield of those bees by using pots and pans. We gathered up some cookware and left to make a stand against a mighty host of bees, with swatters firm in hand.

The string of bees we tracked with ease and once we found the spot, with stealthy steps approached the hole and capped it with a pot. It takes a lot of patience to simply sit and wonder. You want to lift the pot and see what's happening down under! So after half an hour, with both eyes open wide, I stooped to lift the pot off and see what was inside.

Now to our gleeful horror, unveiled before our eyes, we saw a solid ring of bees in a hornet pie! My foolish friend, quite confident, and sure that we had caught them, grabbed her swatter from her belt and then began to swat them!

Of one accord they upward soared and chased us from on high! With screams we raced back home again; I thought that we would die! I learned two life-long lessons which I will now repeat: Never start a project that you cannot complete, and NEVER, NEVER fight a foe that you cannot defeat!

The chicken

The chicken is a humble bird, content to peck the ground, and in *The Book of Chicken Lore* few heroes can be found. No Chicken Valiant, Chicken Kong, nor Chicken Charlemagne, no shining knights, just Chicken Little of inglorious fame! Indeed, it seems remarkable, to some, perhaps appalling: The only claim to chicken fame proclaimed the sky was falling!

And yet this humble little bird does one thing very well: She lays three hundred eggs a year, breakfast in a shell! A good hen lays an egg a day, which seems like quite a feat. From chicken feed to scrambled eggs, now that is hard to beat! But just in case you're unimpressed or quick to underrate it, not all the world's great scientists could ever duplicate it!

But some hens aren't good layers, and these, alas, it's true, will end their days as fryers, or in a chicken stew. And since they're very tasty, it really is no mystery that those who do not earn their pay wind up on a rotisserie!

19

The Crow

The crow is not admired for his feathers nor his song, and yet he makes a lot of noise while others squawk along. He's known to be a scavenger in every land and culture, feasting on dead animals, like buzzards or large vultures.

I read a famous poem once by Edgar Allen Poe, about a stately raven, the cousin to the crow. He must have been a noble bird or come from noble stock, for when the poet stopped to muse, the bird began to talk! While most crows never learn to speak, they're really quite intelligent, with coping skills of cats and dogs and memory of an elephant! And when it comes to getting food, crows are quite resourceful, making tools of grass and twigs to nab a tasty morsel. And crows will eat most anything; it doesn't seem to matter. They'll gobble down a French fry or simply eat the wrapper! They feast on berries, seeds and nuts, and grapes, both green and red, and little things that creep and scurry, both alive and dead.

Farmers try to scare them off. I think you know the reason: They feed on corn and seedlings throughout the growing season. And scarecrows are beneath them, in more ways than just one: They quickly sense they're phonies and even perch on some!

And did you know, they're social birds? They love to flock together, fighting off their enemies and helping one another. And though they don't remember names, they do recall a face, and once attacked will not forget the person nor the place.

Imagine now a million of them flying across the land, with nothing in the vast expanse but miles of desert sand. Tired and in need of rest before the fall of night, they're looking for a place to roost, with not a tree in sight. Then, suddenly, far down below, they spy what look like trees that stretch for miles across the sand as far as eye can see. Sweeping down to earth below, they perch on poles and beams that rise up from the desert sands with phone lines in between. In minutes every phone line is weighted down with crows, and soon the lines begin to sag and touch the lines below.

Now if you think I've made this up, it's true and not a fable, and men have tried all sorts of things to get them off the cables. Now just suppose you're talking on the phone with Mrs. Brown, when suddenly the lines cross and you're heard all over town! Perhaps you might think twice before you talked about a friend, if one day they should answer back on the other end!

All Wound up!

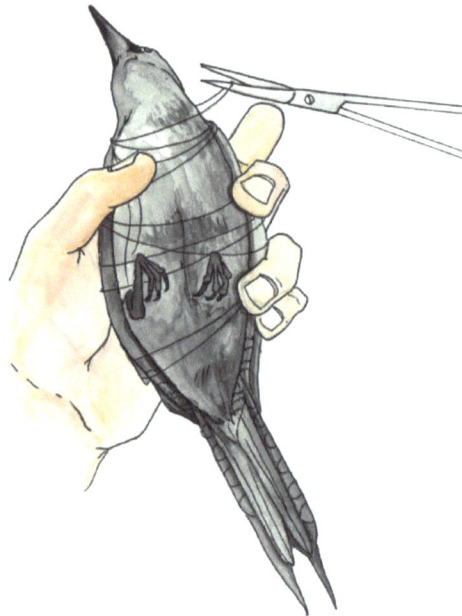

When we were camping near a stream, high up amidst the pines, we came upon a baby crow caught in a fishing line. He couldn't move a muscle and it was clear to me, he'd wrapped himself a hundred times in struggling to get free!

My father gently picked him up and took his army knife, thinking he might cut him free and thus might save his life. It seemed to take forever, so tight was he entwined; he didn't want to cut the bird in snipping off the line. Working very patiently, he cut them one by one. It seemed like half an hour passed before the job was done. And when the final strand was cut, the bird sat in his hands. I wondered if he'd flap his wings or ever fly again.

With care we placed him on the ground, prepared to wait all day, hoping he would show some spunk and try to fly away. So when he flapped his wings and flew, so great was our delight, you'd think we worked for NASA and had launched a satellite!

That didn't happen yesterday, but many years ago, and yet it seems a brief time in the lifespan of a crow. That bird may still be flying, and crows do not forget, but even if he's dead and gone I still remember it! That day I learned a lesson, I hope will follow me: A person kind to helpless things is what I want to be. Not for any glory, nor for men to see, but simply out of gratitude to Him Who cares for me.

22

The Owl

The owl, of all the birds of prey that sweep across the skies, is known in many culturesas dignified and wise. And though by day the eagle reigns supreme among the fowl, by night the monarch of the skies becomes the mighty owl. With eyes aglow he glides o'er fields to spy unwary pests, and when he spots them sweeps them up and flies back to his nest. And unlike hawks that flap their wings with whooshing rush of air, an owl can fly so silently you scarcely know he's there.

His stealthy wings flap up and down and hardly make a sound, allowing him to hear things as they burrow underground. Indeed, with wings so silent and eyes and ears so sharp, he quickly tracks his victims down, even after dark.

While owls can make a lot of sounds and none of them is mute, it may come as a big surprise that some don't give a hoot! Some whistle, hiss or click their tongues, while others squeal and squeak. Still others make a rasping call and all will snap their beak!

I dreamt I was outside one night beneath the starlit skies, when suddenly, up in a tree, appeared a pair of eyes. Then, just as quick, right next to them, I saw a second set, and then a third, and still another, and another yet!

The tree was soon alight with eyes; so many did I see, it felt like standing underneath a giant Christmas tree! And then I heard them start to call, an eerie, haunting hoot, like blowing over bottle tops or softly playing the flute. One by one they all joined in, till soon there were so many, they nearly woke me from my slumber with their hootenanny! Then, suddenly, another sound, much louder than the other: "**Wake up and turn your clock off!**" You're right! It was my mother!

The Woodpecker

Each type of bird is special and in certain ways unique, but one stands out among the rest for his amazing beak. It's not the mighty pelican, though he is special, too, but one that likes to peck on trees to nest and find his food. I'm sure you know the type of bird that I have just described, for woodpeckers can drill more holes than any bird alive! But did you know they're famous for more than just for their beak? They also come with goggle eyes and special gripping feet! Indeed, the "pecking package" includes much more than this: These birds come with a hardened bill and skull that's extra thick. And even then you have to wonder why they don't drop dead! The answer is a cushioned brain and shock absorber head!

But pecking holes in bark for bugs is not for everyone. You need more than a chiseled beak; you need a sticky tongue! Now woodpeckers may disagree, so tell me if I'm wrong, but I have heard that certain ones have tongues four inches long! I wouldn't want to be a bug, for little can they do to fight off tongues like rubber bands tipped with super glue!

But woodpeckers are recognized for more than pecks and taps. They come in vibrant colors, brilliant yellows, reds and blacks. They really are quite beautiful, with endless variations, from ones that measure half a foot to some as big as ravens! And all of them eat other things besides just little bugs; they're also fond of nuts and seeds and tiny worm-like grubs. And some of them have special tastes; they're fond of sucking sap. For them, it's maple syrup without the pancake stack!

Yet even more amazing than all the things they eat, is how they chisel holes in bark with that amazing beak! These birds can peck like hammer-drills, and faster yet, I reckon, pounding on a tree trunk up to twenty times a second! Now if they peck at that rate, and keep it up all day, these birds will peck ten thousand times and still have time to play! I wish my hands could move like that when I sat down to write! I'd finish ten times faster than you could text or type!

If they were pecking doorbells equipped with single chime, before you turned the nob just once they'd ring it twenty times! If someone rang my bell like that, I'd say it was excessive, and maybe now you've come to see, these birds are quite aggressive! It's good that they aren't salesmen, and don't go door to door, for pretty soon they'd be extinct and then there'd be no more!

The Pest Test

My father always taught me, by example more than words, to treat small creatures with respect, from beetles to small birds. He did make one exception for hairy things that hide, like spiders and small rodents that sometimes creep inside. Well, one day his example was sorely tried and tested by a pesky woodpecker that in an oak tree nested.

We lived up in the foothills, amidst the pines and firs, and every day would wake up to the chirping of the birds. While some would sing and others caw, along with every song, we heard a busy woodpecker that hammered off and on. At first he didn't bother us; in fact, we liked the sound. But then, one day, the tree got sick; men came and cut it down. That might not sound like much to you but birds depend on wood, and when that mighty tree came down, he lost his livelihood!

I don't know if a bird's that smart but sometime after that, we heard a pecking on our house; the bird was striking back! We never knew just when he'd strike, nor where he would attack and couldn't get outside in time to catch him in the act.

Now waiting for an air attack can make a person jumpy, and after several weeks of this my dad turned rather grumpy! That crazy bird would come and go and strike us when he pleased, and soon the trim around the house was riddled like Swiss cheese!

JM

26

Before I say another word, allow me to digress, for there's another story here about another pest. Many years before the bird we had a redwood beam that served to hold a clothesline up and also housed some bees. These bees would burrow in the wood and there deposit eggs, which then would hatch and grow to bees and later fly away. Now this was quite a nuisance. Each Spring they'd reappear as if they had a GPS; they came back every year!

My father finally gave up hope of keeping them away, and in frustration cut the post and took the beam away. But bees, though not as smart as us, are nonetheless persistent, and when they couldn't find the beam, they lodged in one more distant.

Now one day it just happened, by chance, or so it seems, my father spied that crazy bird pecking at that beam! He ran and got his pellet gun; his patience had run out. He had to stop that crazy bird from pecking on our house! But when he raised his gun and aimed, a small voice seemed to say: "Why not give him one more chance in hopes he'll go away?" He didn't pull the trigger and let the bird peck on, and when he came back later that pesky thing was gone.

My father passed the test that day, and yet he got his way; that bird flew off into the blue and chose to stay away. And as a "Thank you" bonus, a gift beyond our dreams: Before he left, he pecked out all the bees inside that beam!

27

The Pigeon

Can you name a common bird just smaller than a duck, that bobs its head like chickens do but coos instead of clucks? This bird nests under bridges and on ledges up above, and people sometimes speak of them as "rock" or "turtle doves." Now if you're still uncertain, I'll give you three more clues: This bird will do a courtship dance when he's in love with you! He's known to dwell in palaces of emperors and kings, and when he turns, his neck reflects bright purples, pinks and greens. Did you guess a pigeon? I was thinking that you would! You might have said a rock dove, for that is also good.

Because a pigeon pecks the ground for grain and seed-like pickin's, pigeons are in some ways like their humble friend, the chicken. But chickens are a working bird; they lay an egg a day, while pigeons like the city and the spots where tourists stay. They gather under archways, covered walkways and high eaves, and though you may not see them there, you see the mess they leave! But don't be too preoccupied in watching where you step. Keep an eye on what's above and mind your head and neck!

Yes, pigeon droppings make a mess and they can be a pain, but did you know they once were prized for powers they contain? For centuries men used them to make their plants grow tall and, mixed with other chemicals, to fire cannon balls!

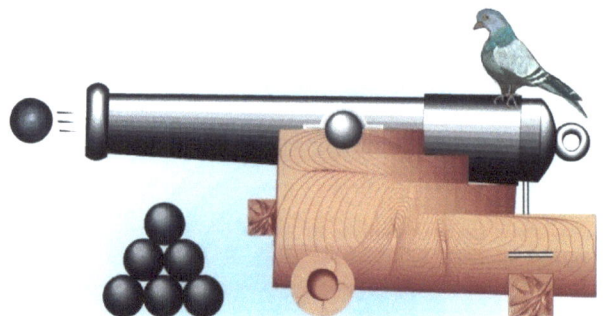

Now doesn't it seem odd to you that eagles stand for power, while doves and pigeons, signs of peace, were used to make gun powder? The next time dove or pigeon droppings pelt you on the head, be thankful they're not cannon balls propelled by them, instead!

Now when you watch them on the ground you might find it amazing that pigeons are so fast in flight, they're often used for racing! Indeed, the fastest fliers move twice as fast as cars and travel up to sixty miles in less than half an hour! And even more impressive, when taken far away, pigeons know their way back home and rarely go astray. Even from great distances and flying all alone, pigeons have a special knack for finding their way home.

Now since they are so speedy, and rarely get confused, men have long relied on them to carry special news. Long before the airplane and emails of our age, pigeons carried messages fastened to their legs. In Roman times and long before these little birds were used to carry scores of sport events and other types of news. Indeed, this common practice achieved such world-wide fame that doves today are still released before Olympic games!

And pigeons are intelligent, as smart as crows, I'll bet. Some can pick out different letters from the alphabet! It isn't any wonder, then, that following the flood, Noah sent out first a raven, then a turtle dove.

They're also good with colors and see things we can't see, so pigeons have been used at times to spot men lost at sea. And while there are a lot of birds more dignified and regal, pigeons have saved far more lives than falcons, hawks and eagles!

We took a trip to Venice once, and stayed near St. Mark's Square. As men in black played violins, we fed the pigeons there. I watched one flutter in the air and gently float back down, as others walked in circles, pecking at the ground. And when they took off like a shot with burst of rapid flaps, it echoed like a theater when people start to clap! The years have come and gone since then and images may fade, but I will not forget those birds, nor memories they made. You might say that their life seems dull, and they seem unaware, but Oh, to be one for a day and live in St. Mark's Square!

G.I. Joe

Pigeons are a common sight; you see them come and go. But one stands out among the rest; they called him "G.I. Joe." Like many soldier pigeons, he flew behind the lines to pick up secret messages and bring them back on time.

Now Joe flew many missions, but one earned world-wide fame, when men were trapped and targeted by bombs from their own planes. The men composed a message and tied it to Joe's leg, then sent him off into the blue to stop the bombing raid.

He flew a mile a minute with not a second lost, and got there as the planes lined up, preparing to take off! I'm glad to say this story came to a happy end, for Joe arrived in time that day to save a thousand men!

The Ostrich

Can you name a nine-foot bird that weighs three hundred pounds? It doesn't fly but lays its eggs in nests carved in the ground. This bird can travel faster and has a longer stride, than almost any horse you'll find and any bird alive! Now if you guessed an ostrich, that's great! You got it right! No other bird in all the world can match its weight and height! Its egg is so much larger than that of any hen, that two could make an omelet for more than twenty men!

Compared to its large body, its legs look rather small, and yet they're placed so perfectly, they wobble not at all. You really have to wonder how any beast so tall can bear such weight on just two legs and never take a fall! But even though its legs are thin, they're like a loaded spring. The ostrich has more bounce per ounce than almost anything! I must confess I'm quite impressed; that's really pretty slick! Three hundred pounds of flesh and feathers perched on pogo sticks!

But should it need to stand and fight, this bird has one more trick: An ostrich leg can kill a lion with a single kick! Indeed, it is surprising, and somehow seems absurd, that ostriches are not included as a nation's bird. Instead, they're often ridiculed, and pictured all around, as somewhat of a stupid bird with head stuck in the ground. And so we often laugh at them for thinking they can hide by simply digging out a hole to stick their head inside! Alas, they are a symbol, without just cause or grounds, of people who refuse to see what's going on around. But ostriches aren't dodos, and when their head is down, it's either to stand out less or turn their eggs around.

JM

31

So when you hear that old refrain of "head stuck in the sand," remember it's an insult to both ostriches and man! And though there really are some folks who seem to act this way, it isn't like an ostrich, no matter what they say!

Now ostrich wings, though very large, are not designed for flight. Instead, they're used as rudders in moving left and right. I wouldn't want to ride this bird, though this is done by some, for fear that I would never know which way it chose to run!

The ostrich is in much demand for meat as well as leather. And who can picture ostriches without those fancy feathers? Nothing can surpass them for their beauty and their luster, and did you know they also make fantastic feather dusters?

The Turkey

I'm thinking of a giant bird that has a bumpy head with flesh that dangles like a rope that's colored crimson red. These birds are multi-colored, with feathers brown to white, and males, like peacocks, fan them out, a most impressive sight! Now while they're rarely raised as pets, they're often in our homes, and cooks may know their inner parts far better than their own. Now if you're feeling baffled, don't worry, that's OK. I'll give you two gigantic clues that might give it away: This bird is very tasty and easy to remember, since every year we roast one, the last week in November. It doesn't chirp like other birds and isn't known for flight*, but can be heard a mile away, gobbling day and night. Did you guess a turkey? You got it right again! But did you know that males and females go by "toms" and "hens?"

Now just in case you're wondering where turkeys got their name, it's taken from the country we know and call the same. Like "Indians," the turkey's name is based upon a quirk: Explorers thought they looked like birds imported by the Turks. Yes, "Indians" and "turkeys" were both named by mistake! They neither come from India nor any foreign state! But names have ways of sticking and once they are applied, it's just as hard get them off as glue when it has dried. And maybe that's a good thing; it's really all the same. It's not the name that makes the man but man that makes the name. They say a rose by any name is really just as sweet, and if that's so it's also true of birds and turkey meat!

While turkeys can't compete with cows that give us milk and hides, they're nonetheless important for products they provide. And when it comes to holidays with all their festive dinners, there is no meat that can compete; the turkey is the winner! Just think of all the

*Wild turkeys do fly, but domestic ones generally are too heavy for flight.

32

things we make with meat that comes from turkeys! There's hamburgers and hot dogs, plus ham and seasoned jerky. It's used in many lunchmeats, from natural to pastrami, and some have even turned it into sausage and salami! Mothers really love it, for reasons more than one: It has less fat than beef and pork and calms you when you're done. Now, after all the candy that's left from *Trick or Treat*, it's nice to have a little trick to put your kids to sleep!

Bur sadly for the turkey, they have their critics, too. Their name is used in insults that people hurl at you. I don't know how to say it, but simply, in a word, turkeys aren't admired for being the brightest bird. Indeed, a lot of other birds are equally maligned, for many insults hurled our way are of the feathered kind. From dodos, loons and cuckoos to chickens, coots and quacks, bird names may be thrown at us, and oft behind our back! But even though the turkey is rather meek and mild, that doesn't means he's dull or dumb, especially in the wild. And though he may not be described as dignified and regal, Ben Franklin deemed the turkey far more noble than the eagle! Now you may laugh and say "No way! That seems to me absurd!" but Franklin also wanted turkeys as our nation's bird. And really, when you think of it, you have to ask "Why not?" They're native to America and do the turkey trot!

But really now, I have to say, not to boast or brag, I'd rather see a regal bird atop our nation's flag. For if I saw a turkey on flagpoles way up high, my stomach might begin to growl for yams and pumpkin pie! And though I do like the turkeys, when all is said and done, I wouldn't want to see their face displayed on Air Force One! And could you hear Neil Armstrong, or men that he commanded, proclaim upon their landing, "The turkey, she has landed?"

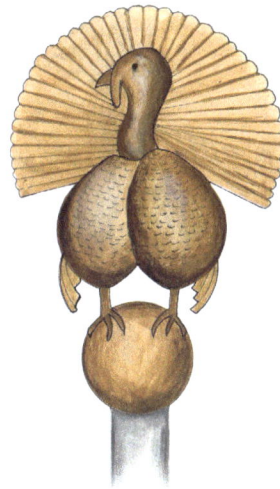

No, turkeys are delicious, and that's what makes them great, but lets keep eagles on our coins and turkeys on our plates! In doing that we'll let the turkey do what it does best: remind us all as citizens of how our nation's blessed!

A Turkey Parade

Turkeys that we raise to eat are far too fat for flight, but wild ones are like pheasants and roost in trees at night. They're not as swift as eagles, but when there is a need, turkeys have been known at times to fly at highway speeds*! And when it comes to running, eagles can't compare; they run at nearly half the speed they travel in the air! Now this is not the type of bird you run across each day, especially near the city, where people choose to stay. Imagine, then, my great surprise when staying in Walnut Creek, I came upon at least a hundred marching down the street! Allow me to back up a bit, for I was far away, and just what I was looking at I really couldn't say. It looked like giant circles stretched out across the street and made me think of farm equipment used to thresh or reap. But when I got up closer, much to my surprise, staring at me, unperturbed, a wall of turkey eyes! And smack dab in the middle, with feathers spread out wide, five gigantic Tom birds, marching side by side! And running all around them, darting left and right, a harem of a hundred hens looking for a bite! There really were much more than that, at least a half again, but since they never stopped to rest, I soon lost track of them. They didn't seem to notice me, standing there alone, and marched along there merry way as I went on my own! The years have come and gone since then and memories may fade, but I will not forget the day I saw those Toms parade! And if you ever have a chance to go to Walnut Creek, you, too, might get to see a few walking down the street!**

*55 mph
**This happened in Rossmoor, a large retirement community that butts up against hills that are full of deer, turkeys and other small animals. To this day you can still see wild turkeys calmly walking the streets amidst cars and people!

Divers and Dippers

The Seal

I'm thinking of an animal that lives in icy seas. He looks and acts much like a dog without the legs or fleas. This animal is popular at circuses and zoos and for a treat will tickle you with tricks that he can do. In case you haven't guessed by now and still are in the dark: You'll sometimes hear the larger ones emit a high-pitched bark. But best of all, they'll make you smile, no matter how you feel. The animal I'm thinking of is called, of course, a seal!

Seals are found around the world, although they're most at home in waters off Antarctica and in the Arctic zone. Some live in the Pacific and may have different names, though all of them are cousins and act a lot the same. Sea lions are massive and carry lots of fat. I guess you'd say they are to seals what cougars are to cats. Add to this, they bark a lot and walk on flipper feet and gather by the thousands on beaches where they meet. Now why they call them lions, I wouldn't want to say, except that some have teeth and manes that make them look that way. The largest seals, called elephants, can weigh four tons and more, making them the heavyweights of all the carnivores. Indeed, these diving monsters can grow to twenty feet, nourished by both sharks and squid and octopi they eat.

Now, seals and all their cousins are known as pinnipeds, which simply means they have winged feet and not a pin-shaped head! Unlike larger pinnipeds that walk upon all fours, seals must wriggle like a worm to inch along the shore. They're really very awkward when moving on the ground, and sometimes do a bounce or roll to get themselves around.

Of course it is no secret that seals are fond of fish, and one of them, the leopard seal, adds penguins to the list. Slender like a serpent and armed with razor teeth, this ten foot penguin predator is one horrific beast! The largest ones are females, and weigh one thousand pounds, not the kind of company a swimmer wants around! And if you are a penguin, you'll need a burst of power, for leopard seals hit speeds of over 20 miles an hour!

And then, there is the walrus, much larger than the seal, that weighs up to four thousand pounds and feasts on mollusk meals. Because their head is very small compared to what's beneath, they rather look like gumdrops with candy canes for teeth. But that's just an illusion, and when you come up close, you'll see they have gigantic tusks the size of three foot posts!

If I could be a circus seal*, that's something I might like. They're handsome, fast and lovable and also super bright. They're favorites at aquariums and stars in water shows, making people laugh a lot at all the tricks they know. And yet, there is a downside to living like a seal. For orcas, sharks and polar bears they make a happy meal. And seals are hunted every year for products they provide: meat and oils from their fat and clothes from pelts and hides. I'm glad some are protected now in certain habitats and species, once endangered, are slowly bouncing back.

In German seals are sea dogs, which seems a fitting name for animals that look like them and often act the same. But even though they act like dogs and can be very sweet, leopard seals are more like wolves that prey upon the weak. I guess that's true of many things that look, at first, alike. We shouldn't judge things by their bark but rather by their bite! No matter if it's dogs and wolves or seals that act like sharks, it's not the outside form that counts but what's inside your heart. Whether you are large or small, a woman or a man, you can be most anything if you think you can. And if you are courageous and true to what you feel, who knows, you might grow up one day to be a Navy SEAL!

*Circus seals are really sea lions.   37

The Turtle

Of all the world's great creatures, the turtle is unique, the only living reptile with retracting head and feet! Now that is all made possible by one amazing fact: The turtle always travels with a roof upon his back! Perhaps that's why he's plodding and moves so very slow, for truly he's an animal that takes his home in tow. Other beasts are lighter, and therefore very swift, while turtles, by comparison, have got a lot to lift!

Turtles form a family that is large and quite diverse: about three hundred types in all spread out around the earth. They live in warmer climates, in oceans and on land, and range in size from mattresses to ones that fit your hand. Leatherbacks, the largest, can weigh two thousand pounds and swim in every ocean where jellyfish are found. They really love to travel, which might explain their smile. In just one year a leatherback will go ten thousand miles!

Turtles are endearing, as gentle as you'll find unless, of course, you are a fish and meet the snapping kind. His worm-like tongue works like a lure, his mouth an open trap, and when a fish draws very near it closes with a SNAP! You wouldn't want to pet one, not even in a zoo, for when his jaws come snapping shut he'll break a broom in two!

Now some call turtles "tortoises." I'm sure you've heard both names. But even though they look alike, they're really not the same. Tortoises are turtles, or in the turtle clan, but turtles live in water and tortoises on land. Turtles come with paddle feet or fins to help them swim, while tortoises have stubby toes attached to walking limbs. While tortoises find plants and shrubs to be a tasty dish, turtles feed on many things, including clams and fish. Both are known as reptiles, which means they hatch from eggs, and unlike frogs and pollywogs they're born with all their legs. Neither one is social—they're happiest alone—protected in their "castle shell" which also is their home. Turtles have a streamlined shell of green and earthen tones, while tortoises are housed, instead, in shells that look like domes. Though both can live for many years, a tortoise is well known for going past a hundred years and never leaving home!

I'm sure you've heard the story of the tortoise and the hare. When challenged to a race one day, the tortoise took the dare. And since he never paused to rest nor ever slacked his pace, the tortoise, moving slow but sure, went on to win the race. And though a hare is faster, that doesn't mean he's stronger. The wise old tortoise takes it slow and lives a whole lot longer!

I think that there's a moral here, so take it if you can: Some who start out very well don't end like they began. I liken them to flashbulbs, "flashes in the pan," brilliant at the starting line with nothing in the end. So while it's very noble to start out swift and fast, I'd rather be a turtle, slow but built to last. And if this seems pure sentiment, I don't think I'm alone, for turtles are a favorite pet in many hearts and homes.

The Penguin

Can you name a giant bird whose wings aren't meant for flight, that waddles like a giant duck and stands and walks upright? He wears a little jacket of black upon pure white. If you guessed a penguin, you're absolutely right!

The penguin is a funny bird, never meant to fly, and yet he moves through water like eagles soar through sky. And though his wings aren't made for flight he flaps them with such flair, that when he leaves water, he shoots into the air!

Other birds are hatched from eggs in nests perched way up high, so when they topple to the earth they flap their wings and fly. Penguins, though, are hatched from eggs that line the water's rim, so when they fall into the waves they flap their wings and swim! Because their walk is awkward and movement rather slow, they'll often go tobogganing by sliding on the snow.

39

But when they hit the water, the switch is automatic, from snow-bird to sensation in water acrobatics! And though, when out of water, their eyesight is quite weak, their hearing can discern between a thousand different peeps! No matter what the number of nestlings in their midst, each bird can find its baby by the sound that it emits!

I wouldn't be a penguin, though I might on one condition: They place me in a comfy zoo where people pay admission! I couldn't brave the freezing cold nor fish for every meal, nor sit in darkness six months long and deal with leopard seals. I'd rather have an easy life, footloose and fancy free, and laugh at all the funny faces staring back at me!

The Beaver

Can you name an animal that gnaws wood like a rat and topples giant fir trees to change his habitat? An animal with silky fur that trappers used to catch to make their fortune selling pelts for clothing and for hats? In case you haven't guessed by now I'll give you one more clue: This animal lives on the land and in the water, too. Did you guess a beaver? I was thinking that you might! I'm taking off my hat to you; you're absolutely right!

Beavers are a rodent, which means they like to gnaw, and given time they'll fell more trees than men with ax and saw! Starting with a rippling stream and two or three felled logs, they soon construct a dam or dyke that doubles as a lodge. Now many birds and animals will build a little nest, but when it comes to building homes the beaver is the best! No other type of animal can match the house he builds. The largest stretches longer than seven football fields!

How is it that the beaver, with teeth his only tool, is able to construct a dam and make a swimming pool? Now some folks, when they can't explain what they've seen or heard,

40

may simply call it "instinct," or invent another word. Others say he builds a dam for food and for protection, but who, pray tell, alerts him to move in this direction? I find it quite amazing that he thinks to build a pool when he hasn't ever seen it done nor gone to beaver school!

Now beavers form a family that is caring and close-knit, in which the older children help their parents with the "kits." And while the younger beavers are engaged in play and frolic, the older, more mature ones slave away like workaholics!

Sometimes when you see them swim, with head above the water, it's easy to mistake them for their look-alike, the otter. Now while the two share many traits and seem in some ways equal, beavers are like river rats, and otters, water weasels.

Beavers feed on plants and trees and other herbal treats, while otters are carnivorous and feast on fish and meat. And otters have four canine teeth, quite unlike the beaver, whose razor sharp incisors work like timber cleavers. Another thing that makes a beaver different from an otter: He has a tail that's long and flat with which he slaps the water. It helps to keep him upright and works just like a rudder that turns in four directions to guide him through the water.

Yes, beavers are amazing but I wouldn't want to be one, for making and repairing dams seems absolutely NO fun. While bears are always hungry and cats laid-back and easy, beavers seem to gain their fame by always being busy! Now add to that the funny fact they're also known as "eager," for the simple reason that it rhymes with "busy beaver!" And yet that might not be so bad, and some will even say: "What counts as work for one man is another person's play."

Beavers at Play

Farewell

I hope you liked these stories and learned some lessons, too! Most of what I said in them is based on what is true. And though it wasn't always fun when each one came to pass, I have to say, on looking back, I sometimes smile or laugh. Now, if I missed your animal, there's something you can do: Read about as many more in Animals, Book 2!

www.ingramcontent.com/pod-product-compliance
Lightning Source LLC
Chambersburg PA
CBHW042058040426
42448CB00002B/61